Contents

Historical time is divided into two major periods. BC is short for "before Christ" – that is, the time before the Christian religion began. This is the time up to the year 1 BC. AD is short for "Anno Domini". This is Latin for "in the year of our Lord", meaning the time from the year 1 BC to the present. For example, when the calendar says the year is AD 1000, it is 1000 years after the year 1 BC. The abbreviation c. stands for *circa*, which is Latin for "around".

Any words appearing in the text in bold, **like this**, are explained in the glossary.

Why do we play?

People of all ages like to play games. We play games for fun and to compete: everyone likes to win! Games can teach, too. They help us practise skills, such as how to add up, spell, or follow rules. Physical games – for example, hopscotch – teach body skills such as jumping and throwing. Dolls and toy animals teach children to **role-play** and care for things.

Children often have a favourite teddy bear. This bear was made in 1904.

Popular toys and games have changed over time. The timeline in this book will show you how toys have developed. New materials and new **manufacturing** processes bring new toy inventions to the shops. Different toys can be popular in different countries. People's toys and games are influenced by their **culture**, taste, and wealth.

Computer games are quite a new invention. This Nintendo DS game **console** was available worldwide in 2009.

TIMELINE HISTORY

GAMES

From Dice to Gaming

Liz Miles

www.raintreepublishers.co.uk
Visit our website to find out more information about Raintree books.

To order:

☎ Phone 0845 6044371

🖹 Fax +44 (0) 1865 312263

🖾 Email myorders@raintreepublishers.co.uk

Customers from outside the UK please telephone +44 1865 312262

Raintree is an imprint of Capstone Global Library Limited, a company incorporated in England and Wales having its registered office at 7 Pilgrim Street, London, EC4V 6LB – Registered company number: 6695582

Edited by Louise Galpine and Diyan Leake
Designed by Richard Parker
Original illustrations © Capstone Global Library Ltd 2011
Illustrated by Jeff Edwards (map, p. 5) and Darren Lingard (card suits, p. 11)
Picture research by Hannah Taylor
Originated by Dot Gradations Ltd
Printed and bound in China by CTPS

ISBN 978 0 431 02556 8 (hardback)
14 13 12 11 10
10 9 8 7 6 5 4 3 2 1

British Library Cataloguing in Publication Data
Miles, Liz – Games : from dice to gaming. – (Timeline history)
795-dc22
A full catalogue record for this book is available from the British Library.

Acknowledgements
We would like to thank the following for permission to reproduce photographs: akg-images pp. **6** (Erich Lessing), **13** top (Alameda Films/Real Madrid TV/Transglobe Pictures/Wanda Films/Album), **14** bottom; Alamy Images pp. **9** top (© David Hancock), **10** bottom (© Interfoto), **11** (© The London Art Archive), **12** (© Jake Lyell), **22** top (©Interfoto), **23** top (© Jon Bower Thailand), **24** bottom (© Jenny Matthews), **26** (© StockImages), **27** (© Network Photographers); Corbis pp. **7** bottom (Jack Fields), **13** bottom (Francis G. Mayer), **15** bottom (Oliver Weiken), **16** bottom (National Archives/Science Faction), **20** top (BBC), **20** bottom (Hulton-Deutsch Collection), **22** bottom (Klaus Hackenberg), **25** (Philippe Lissac); Getty Images pp. **4** top (AFP/John D. McHugh), **9** bottom (Michael Springer), **21** (AFP/John D. McHugh), **23** bottom (Time & Life Pictures/Ralph Morse), **24** top (Bill Greenblatt); istockphoto p. **17** top (© Vladimir Ovchinnikov); Photolibrary pp. **8** (Peter Holmes), **19** (Jose Fuste Raga); Rex Features pp. **4** bottom (Etienne Ansotte), **18** bottom (Nils Jorgensen); Rijksmuseum p. **14** top; The Art Archive pp. **7** top (Kanellopoulos Museum Athens/Dagli Orti), **16** top (Musée des Arts Africains et Oceaniens/Dagli Orti), TopFoto p. **15** top); © V&A Images/Victoria and Albert Museum, London pp. **10** top, **18** top.

Cover photograph of a trade show for computer and video games reproduced with permission of Alamy Images (© Jochen Tack).

We would like to thank Bill Marriott for his invaluable help in the preparation of this book.

Every effort has been made to contact copyright holders of material reproduced in this book. Any omissions will be rectified in subsequent printings if notice is given to the publisher.

Timelines

The information in this book is on a timeline. A timeline shows you events in the order they happened in history. The big timeline in the middle of each page gives you details of a certain time in history (see below).

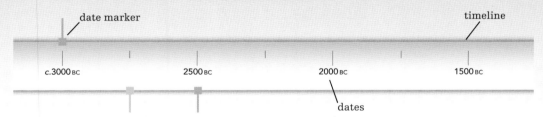

Some dates are exact. For example, the first talking doll was invented in the year 1823. Others are more general because people may not have kept written records or the event happened over a period of time. The smaller timeline at the bottom of each page shows you how the page you are reading fits into history as a whole. You will read about games from all around the world. Each entry on the main timeline is in a different colour. This colour shows you which continent the information is about. The map below shows you how this colour coding works. Pale green indicates events that took place on more than one continent or worldwide.

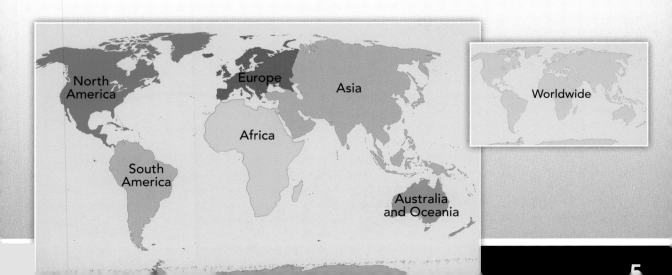

Ancient beginnings

Some of our toys and games were played thousands of years ago. They were handmade from simple materials such as wood, stone, **terracotta**, and metal.

*c.*3000 BC

A board game similar to **draughts** was played in Mesopotamia (an area we now call Iraq). This stone board, 14 pieces, and 3 dice were found buried in a royal tomb.

3000 BC	2500 BC	2000 BC	1500 BC

*c.*3000–1800 BC

Ancient Egyptians played with stone marbles.

*c.*2500 BC

The ancient Indus Valley **civilizations** left behind toys such as clay animals on wheels.

c.500 BC

Ancient Greek texts describe yo-yos made from metal, wood, and painted terracotta. This Greek warrior toy is made from terracotta.

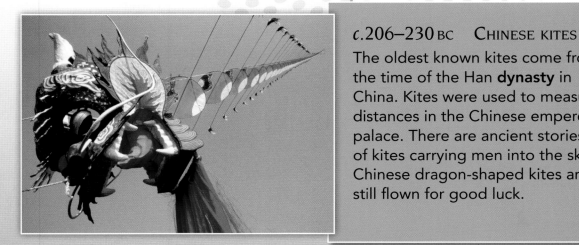

c.206–230 BC CHINESE KITES

The oldest known kites come from the time of the Han **dynasty** in China. Kites were used to measure distances in the Chinese emperor's palace. There are ancient stories of kites carrying men into the sky. Chinese dragon-shaped kites are still flown for good luck.

1000 BC   500 BC   1 BC

Toys as tools

When **archaeologists** find old toy-like objects, they cannot be sure if they were made just for play. Some old "toys" were made for other purposes.

AD 286–476

In ancient Rome, boys had small bows and arrows. They practised shooting arrows as training to be good soldiers. Boys played a game similar to today's hopscotch, too, perhaps to improve their hand and foot skills.

| AD 250 | AD 300 | AD 350 | AD 400 | AD 450 |

c. AD 300

Adults often played games just for fun. The Indian game of pachisi was played by emperors and princes. It was a board game like the ludo that is played today (right). Small shells were thrown instead of dice.

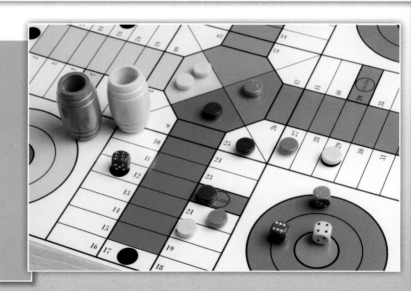

AD 325–925

The Mayan **civilization** made "worry dolls". They were lucky charms, not toys. Today people tell their worries to these dolls. They hope the dolls will take the worries away.

AD 500 | AD 550 | AD 600 | AD 650 | AD 700

c. AD 700 KACHINA DOLLS

Native American Hopi people carved kachina dolls to look like the gods from their myths (stories of ancient gods and heroes). Parents used kachina dolls to teach the stories to their children.

Remember the rules!

Games with complicated rules were played all around the world. For example, players had to remember how different game pieces moved and what cards to play.

AD 600

People in India played a game called chaturanga. Over time it became the game we know as chess. The pieces were characters such as king, queen, horses, elephants, chariots, and foot soldiers.

AD 600   AD 700   AD 800   AD 900

AD 1100

Chess was very popular in the Middle Ages. These chess pieces from the 1100s are carved out of walrus tusk. They were found on the Isle of Lewis in Scotland.

c. AD 1280 ALFONSO'S BOOK

King Alfonso X of Spain put together the first book of games played in Europe (*Libro de Juegos*). It describes the rules of games. Many of the games in Alfonso's book came from overseas, such as nine men morris from Egypt and backgammon and chess from India, shown here.

1000	1100	1200	1300

AD 1300

By this time, Egyptians were playing with decks of cards similar to today's. There were 52 cards and 4 or 5 suits (sets of pictures). The suits included coins, swords, staffs, and cups.

AD 1300

The Maori of New Zealand played cat's cradle, making patterns by twisting a single piece of string between their hands.

Balls, bones, and stones

Ready-made games such as chess were only for the very wealthy. Ordinary people still made their own toys or played games that needed nothing at all except for the players.

1450s

African tribes played a game which is still played today. It has a board of small holes carved into planks of wood or dug in the ground. The two players try to capture each other's pieces, which are stones or dried seeds or beans. The game has different names in different part of Africa. One of the names is hus.

1440   1460   1480   1500

1500s

Shove-groat was a popular game in **taverns** in Shakespeare's England. A groat was a coin. Players had to shove coins along a table to reach special marks. It is still played today and is called shove-ha'penny.

1500s

When Spanish explorers reached America they saw people playing with a rubber ball for the first time. The Mayan **civilizations** used sap from trees to make the first balls that bounced.

1520   1540   1560

1560   BLADDER BALLS

This painting from 1560 shows that most children did not need much to have fun. They played leapfrog or used wooden sticks and hoops. Balls in Europe were made from a range of things, from animal **bladders** to skulls. The bladders were blown up. The game of **knucklebones** used animal bones!

Who played with this?

Many toys and games were enjoyed by a certain group of people. For example, expensive dolls' houses were a favourite toy among rich European women.

1600s

The first dolls' houses were made for adults, not children. Wealthy women in the 1600s paid craftsmen to make them.

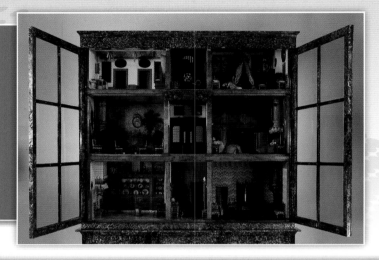

1600   1635   1670

1613

Dutch **settlers** were the first to play skipping games in North America. But only men played them. People worried that girls might hurt themselves!

1700s

A board game called mancala has been played for thousands of years. By the 1700s, it was played (mainly by adults) throughout Africa and Asia.

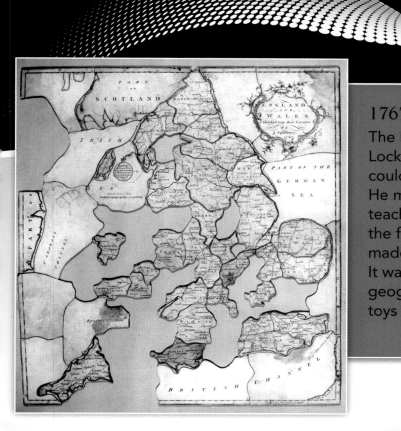

1767 TOYS TO TEACH

The English **philosopher** John Locke (1632–1704) believed toys could be used as a teaching aid. He made some letter blocks to teach boys the alphabet. One of the first jigsaw puzzles (left) was made in 1767 for schoolchildren. It was of a map used to teach geography. Jigsaws became toys in the 1820s.

1705

1740

1775

1700s

At first, **pedlars** in China used a diabolo to attract people to see their wares. In Europe, diabolo became a game for the upper classes. It is still used today in China for exercise to keep fit.

Toy revolution

During the **Industrial Revolution**, factories began **mass-producing** toys in England, then Europe and North America. Mass-production made toys cheaper. There were also new materials and inventions, such as talking dolls.

1800s

Changes in **manufacturing** did not reach Africa so quickly. Most toys were still homemade. This doll from Cameroon was made in the 1800s from wood, beads, and shells.

1800   1820   1840

1823 Crawling and talking dolls

The first talking doll was made by a German inventor. The doll said, "Ma-ma" and "Pa-pa". Lifting an arm worked bellows (air-filled bags) inside, which made the sounds. Inventors started to make moving dolls, too. Pins and cogs, like those inside a clock, made dolls walk and crawl. The doll in the picture was made in the 1870s.

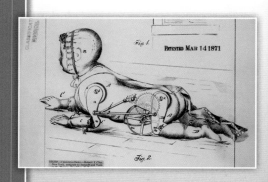

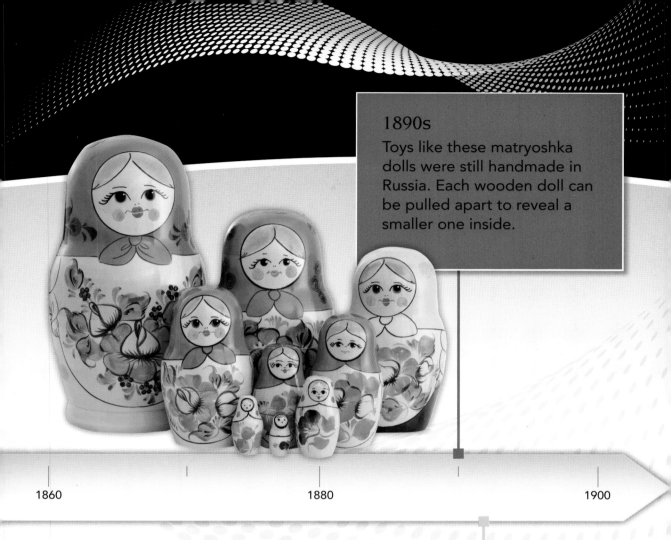

1890s

Toys like these matryoshka dolls were still handmade in Russia. Each wooden doll can be pulled apart to reveal a smaller one inside.

1860

1880

1900

1892

The ancient Indian game of snakes and ladders became popular in England. It was used to teach children how to behave, as counters went up a ladder when they came to a "good" square and down a snake when they came to a "bad" one.

Big names

The toy industry grew, and companies such as Steiff, Parker Brothers, and John Waddington made lots of money.

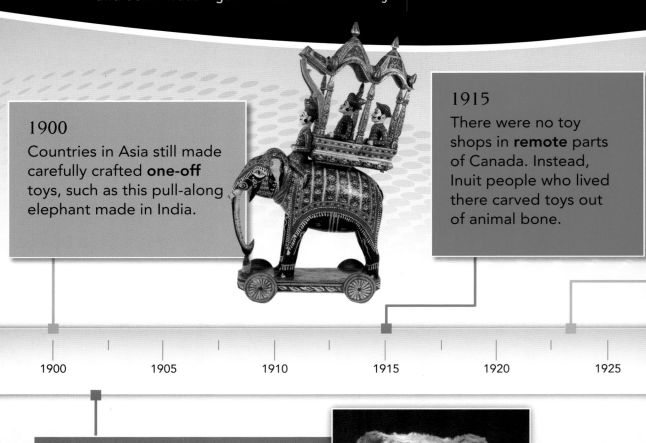

1900

Countries in Asia still made carefully crafted **one-off** toys, such as this pull-along elephant made in India.

1915

There were no toy shops in **remote** parts of Canada. Instead, Inuit people who lived there carved toys out of animal bone.

1900   1905   1910   1915   1920   1925

1902

The German company Steiff made their first toy bear. Every Steiff toy has a little button in its ear to prove it is made by Steiff. People in the United States named toy bears after their president, "Teddy" (short for Theodore) Roosevelt.

1920s

The first **pachinko** machine was made in Japan. It became such a popular game that rows of adults now **gamble** on them in places called pachinko parlours.

1949

The Danish company Lego sold the first famous fit-together plastic bricks. Six Lego bricks can fit together in at least 102,981,500 different ways.

1930 1935 1940 1945 1950

1935 CLEVER INVENTIONS

Parker Brothers brought out Monopoly. The "money-making" board game helped Americans to forget their poverty in the **Great Depression**. In the 1940s a game called Candy Land was invented. It was popular as a way of "giving children sweets" without the bad effects of eating real sweets.

1948

The word game Scrabble went on sale. More than 100 million sets have been sold worldwide.

I saw it on TV!

In the 1950s some of the first television programmes were made for children. The viewers wanted games linked to the programmes. Advertisements encouraged people to buy games.

1950

A popular television programme called *Andy Pandy* was first shown in the UK. Toy versions of the characters went on sale.

1950   1952   1954   1956

1950s

Toys such as this Australian koala were often covered in real animal fur. Soon factory-made fibres such as **nylon** and polyester replaced animal fur. It was more **hygienic**, cheaper, and ensured no animal was killed to make the toy.

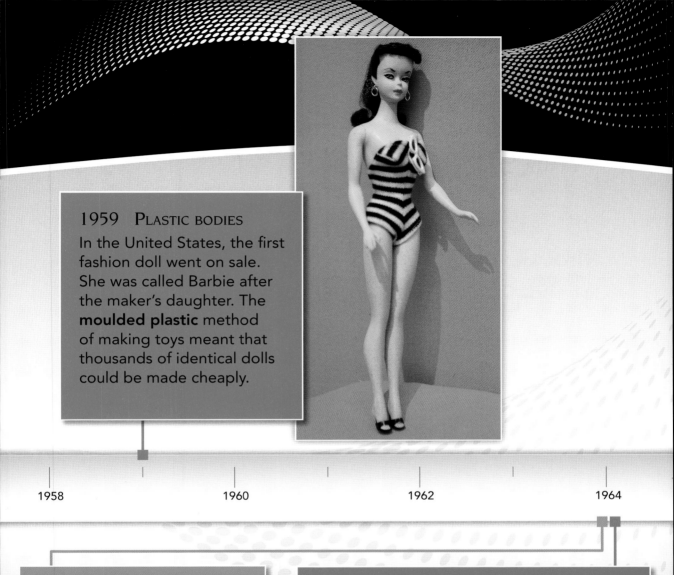

1959 PLASTIC BODIES

In the United States, the first fashion doll went on sale. She was called Barbie after the maker's daughter. The **moulded plastic** method of making toys meant that thousands of identical dolls could be made cheaply.

1958   1960   1962   1964

Mid-1960s

A New Zealand company started to make metal car models. It was part of a worldwide craze. More families owned cars, so more children wanted toy cars to play with.

1964

The first G.I. Joe "action figure" was made for boys in the United States. In the United Kingdom, it was called Action Man. Some people thought that **military** toys encouraged children to be violent.

Crazes

New toys came and went, depending on the latest craze. Just before Christmas in 1984 all the cloth dolls called Cabbage Patch Kids were sold out, but in 1986 everyone wanted a Transformer.

1970s COMPUTER FIRSTS

Nintendo, a company in Japan, released the first colour TV **video game**. Players used paddles to hit a ball. The first popular game was Pong, made by Atari in 1972. It was a tennis-style game played on a TV screen (right). The computer craze grew in 1989 when Nintendo released **Game Boy**.

| 1970 | 1971 | 1972 | 1973 | 1974 | 1975 |

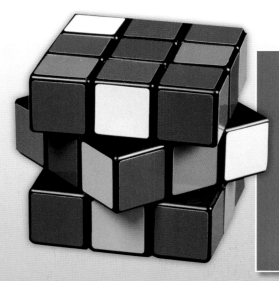

1975

The puzzle called Rubik's Cube was named after its inventor, a Hungarian professor named Ernö Rubik. The puzzle can be moved into 43,252,003,274,489,856,000 different arrangements, but only one is right!

1980s

In **remote** rural places, many children did not (and still do not) have modern toys. This Indonesian child is playing on stilts made from local plants.

1976   1977   1978   1979   1980

1977

After the movie *Star Wars* came out, *Star Wars* **merchandise** sold well. More money was made from *Star Wars* books and toys than from the film itself.

Collect the set!

International advertising makes toys popular worldwide. Clever **marketing**, such as making sure items are rare, encourages people to want whole series of toys or cards all the more.

1990s
Nine types of Beanie Babies were launched. Later, more of these bean-bag animals were made. Only a few were made of some types, to keep them rare.

| 1990 | 1992 | 1994 | 1996 | 1998 | 2000 |

1997
The Pokémon Card Trading Game was released, based on a **video game** from Japan. It was invented by Satoshi Tajiri, whose idea for the "pocket monster" cards and pictures came from his love of collecting bugs as a boy.

2006 HERE WII GO!

New video game **consoles** produced realistic moving pictures. They were Microsoft's Xbox 360, Sony's PlayStation 3, and Nintendo's Wii. Wii (pronounced *wee*) lets you play a sport such as tennis in your lounge! The console picks up the way you move a special racket or **remote control**. Wii Sports is marketed as a way of keeping fit.

2002		2004		2006		2008		2010	

2005

Kite fighting was banned in Pakistan. For fighting, kites are attached to wire covered in powdered glass. The wire is used to cut away opponents' kites. The sharp wires had injured people.

Good and bad

Many parents worry that today's popular computer games keep children indoors too much and stop them from playing together. Even board games can now be played by a child alone, using a computer.

Present
This is a game of chess played on a computer.

People also worry that cheap plastic toys use up too many resources, and the world's resources are running out.

Traditional toys

The answer to these worries might be to play more traditional games, such as hopscotch and skipping. They are healthier and use fewer resources. But many children will always want the latest toy or best computer **console**. And computer games can stimulate the mind and help with **dexterity**.

Present

Many children are too poor to buy toys or computer games. They make their own games. These children in Brazil have made a **draughts** set using bottle tops.

Safety

Toy safety is important, too. If the paint used on toys contains lead, this can cause poisoning that may harm a child's brain. Toys may have small parts that can come loose and cause problems if children swallow them. Many countries have passed laws to make toys safe.

Key dates

c.3000–1800 BC
Ancient Egyptians play with stone marbles.

c.206–230 BC
People in China use kites to measure distances.

c. AD **300**
People in India play pachisi, which is a game like ludo.

AD **600**
People in India play a game called chaturanga, which becomes the game we know as chess.

1280
King Alfonso X of Spain puts together the first book of games in Europe.

1300
The Maori of New Zealand play cat's cradle.

1450s
African tribes play hus. The two players try to capture each other's pieces, which are stones or dried seeds or beans.

1500s
The Mayan **civilizations** use sap from rubber trees to make the first balls that bounce.

1600s
The first dolls' houses are made.

1760s
The first jigsaw puzzles are made for schoolchildren.

1823
The first talking doll is made by a German inventor.

1892
The ancient Indian game of snakes and ladders becomes popular in England.

1948
The word game Scrabble goes on sale.

1959
The Barbie doll goes on sale.

1975
The Rubik's Cube is invented. The puzzle can be moved into 43,252,003,274,489,856,000 different arrangements.

2006
New **video game consoles** produce realistic moving pictures. These are Microsoft's Xbox 360, Sony's PlayStation 3, and Nintendo's Wii.

Glossary

archaeologist person who studies what has been left behind from the past. Future archaeologists might dig up one of your old toys.

bladder a bag-like organ in the body. Animal bladders can be blown up like a balloon.

civilization particular society or culture at a particular period of time

console small box or panel of controls

culture customs and beliefs that a group of people has

dexterity skill with your hands

draughts a game for two players, played on a chequered board

dynasty ruling family

gamble make a bet that something will happen in the hope of making money

Game Boy small, battery-powered video game system

Great Depression period in the 1930s when money lost its value and many people were poor

hygienic completely clean and won't make people ill

Industrial Revolution time of sweeping change when masses of people moved from farming into industry

knucklebones game in which you throw and catch small bones or other objects with one hand

manufacture make something, usually in a factory

marketing making people aware of things to buy

mass-produce make things in large quantities

merchandise goods linked to a film or book

military to do with the armed forces

moulded plastic plastic that is formed by pouring it into shapes, called moulds

nylon a strong fabric made from chemicals

one-off item that is unlike any other item

pachinko a game in which a ball whizzes round into a hole

pedlar person who travels around selling things

philosopher someone who tries to work out the meaning of life

remote far away from other people and difficult to reach

remote control box that controls a device from a distance

role-play act as if you are someone else

settler person who goes to live in a different land

tavern drinking house. Today we call taverns pubs or bars.

terracotta clay that has been heated to make pottery

video game electronic or computerized game

Find out more

Books

Ancient Olympic Games **(The Olympics series)**, Haydn Middleton (Heinemann Library, 2008)

Cricket **(Know Your Sport series)**, Chris Oxlade (Franklin Watts, 2006)

Sport Files series (Raintree, 2008)

Welcome to the Ancient Olympics!, Jane Bingham (Heinemann Library, 2007)

Would You Believe ... the Losers Were Killed in Mayan Football?: and Other Perilous Pastimes, Richard Platt (Oxford University Press, 2007)

Websites

Learn lots of different ways to play hopscotch:
home.howstuffworks.com/hopscotch-games.htm

Find out about record-holders in a range of sports and games on the Guinness World Records website:
www.guinnessworldrecords.com/records/sports_and_games

More about the famous bear company, Steiff:
www.steiffteddybears.co.uk/steiff_interest.asp

Places to visit

Pollock's Toy Museum

1 Scala Street

London W1T 2HN

Tel: 020 7636 3452

V&A Museum of Childhood

Cambridge Heath Road

London E2 9PA

Tel: 020 8983 5200

http://www.vam.ac.uk

Index